WELCOME TO YOUR
Life By Design Journal

When I think back on my life, way before I became a professional coach, while I was just a little girl beginning at age 10, while in school, into college, during my first *AND* second marriage, as a mother of three, and now six... as a sister, a daughter, a friend... I see the simple act of journaling was my constant.
I am a talker by nature and when no one is around to listen,
I become a writer by default.
Better out than in they say!
As a result, I realized the ritual and practice of writing down my own thoughts, reflections and dreams has been **THE** essential self-care tool to
designing my life!

Life By Design. I Love Mine.

That is why I designed this journal for **YOU**.
The question I have for you now is, do you love **YOUR life**?

This self-care coaching journal will provide you with self coaching prompts developed from my 25+ years of professional coaching experience. It is designed to make you think, feel and reflect in perhaps different ways than you ever have before so that you, too, can love your **life by design**!

Before you know it, this simple self-guided set of exercises will become your foundational practice for attracting your deepest heart's desires
...or something even better.

Happy Designing,

XOXO
Your Coach, Nicoa

HOW TO USE YOUR
Life By Design Journal

Three Easy Steps To A Life By Design You Love:

- **STEP ONE:** Read the self-care guidance and weekly prompts. Sit with the topic for a moment and just mull it over in your mind. Reflect on what comes up for you. *PAUSE.* **Be the observer of you. Listen to your inner voice for a moment.**

- **STEP TWO:** Turn to your *Journaling* **pages** and start writing. Reflect on how the self-care information and prompts make you feel energetically, emotionally & somatically (*physically*). Write whatever comes to mind. Is there something coming up that you now need or want to do going forward? What? With Whom? Any initial thoughts of How? When? Why? **Write that down!** All of it!

- **STEP THREE:** Start **DESIGNING** the vision of that future related to your ideas and actions from the prompt. ***What do you really want now?*** Write the response to this question in as much detail as possible. **Use all of your senses**: colors, sounds, tastes, smells... include timing, material items, people, locations and, most importantly, how receiving and experiencing **ALL OF THIS** into your life will make you *FEEL*! That's it. That's all you have to do!

Remember, this is **YOUR** self-guided journaling practice and my intention by creating it for you is to help you help yourself understand where you are now in your life in order to define and design a **life you love...**
the kind of life you don't need a vacation from!
Congratulations. You're one step closer.

Life by design. I love mine. You can love yours, too.

Life By Design Journal

TIPS

- First of all, you deserve to take time for yourself to reflect. Savor it.
- Remember that these journal prompts aren't required, they are just to get you thinking, and feeling. Use them...or not, but write anyway!
- Sit somewhere that makes you feel comfortable and relaxed whenever possible, but don't let location prevent you from journaling.
- Use your favorite pen, pencil,...draw pictures or doodle, too. The mind only responds to words AND images. You may prefer to type this online, that's an option, too.
- Wish to have an accompanying beverage? That might be nice. I prefer coffee!
- How about some soothing background music? Hey Siri? Alexa?
- Perhaps change your clothes so you also feel comfortable in your own skin as you are journaling. I prefer my comfy yoga clothes, and a favorite blanket!
- Need to tell someone that you need some privacy and wish to not be disturbed? In person, via text, or a note on the door? Boundaries. You deserve it.
- Remember, this journal is yours to use as you wish. There are no wrong or right entries, only you know what feels good and what matters most to you in your process. No one is grading this! Your life, your design!
- Lastly, give yourself permission to surrender into the moment and allow yourself to enjoy the process of getting to know yourself, and your life, better. Yes, this is "the work" as they say, but remember, you can't design it if you don't define it. Now, it's time to get going!

It's your Life By Design!

SETTING THE GROUND WORK

What are the some of the main reasons you made this investment in yourself? What's your WHY?

_____
_____
_____
_____
_____
_____
_____

How will you hold yourself accountable to writing in this journal regularly? Do you like a routine or flow?

_____
_____
_____
_____
_____
_____
_____

How will you know this investment in yourself was worth it? What will life look like after doing this work?

_____
_____
_____
_____
_____

Understanding Real Self-Care

Self-care is an essential **practice** that encompasses all aspects of our lives. It involves taking care of our *physical, emotional, and mental health*. Self-care is not a luxury but a necessity. Some people often think of self-care as selfish. I disagree. I think **self-care is NOT selfish, it is strategic!**
And not only is it strategic, it is critical to a life you love.

But what is self-care really? That's what this journal aims to clarify for you as you reflect and create your life by design.

Strategic self-care begins with a process of identifying your needs and finding ways to meet those needs in your day to day life. Ideally in a state of flow, with the least amount of resistance or compartmentalizing. When you prioritize taking care of yourself, first, you are better equipped to handle the challenges that life throws at you with more ease, grace and fulfillment. That's the whole point right, **fulfillment?**
A happy, satisfying life?

How's that working for you lately?

Strategic self-care can take many forms, including physical activities like exercise, taking care of our nourishment, getting enough quality sleep, and taking breaks from work and life obligations but it also has to do with your way of Being. Tending to your soul! Intentionally designing emotional activities like spending time with loved ones, practicing mindfulness, **journaling!**, and seeking therapy or coaching can be just some of the ways to foster a strategic self-care approach prioritizing **YOU**.
Here's the thing, this life of yours? It is whatever you decide it is!

I invite you to keep in mind, too, that strategic self-care is heavily steeped in self-awareness, radical honesty and authentic truth-telling with yourself and others. Being truthful when requesting what you want and authentically co-creating a life by design, on **YOUR terms**, is the outcome we're seeking with this journal. Your terms are those you will uncover, remember and rediscover through this process. Terms that align with your true values and standards. If it matters to you, then you deserve to create practices to attract everything that you want and crave in your life.

Unapologetically.

JOURNAL PROMPT

It's not hard to make decisions when you know what your values are.
— Roy E. Disney

Whose life are you living? Yours or your parents, or societies?
Have you ever asked yourself what truly matters most to you?
What are your values and standards in life?

Research tells us that the majority of people are living their life by default and not by design. They don't know where their life is headed, and they don't have a plan for what they want to accomplish in life.

On a scale of 1-10, how satisfied are you in your life? In your career? In your intimate relationships?

It's time to take action to ensure you are living YOUR life on your own terms.

When you know what truly matters to you, then every action, every reaction, and every interaction naturally aligns to just that.
You know, like you know, like you know.

Your Life By Design

JOURNAL PROMPT

What do you think is more sustainable, self-sacrifice or self-care? Self-sacrifice is putting others needs before your own, while self-care is putting your needs first. Which is your default tendency?

Self-prioritizing happens when you align your habits and your boundaries in life. Do not confuse it with neglecting others around you that you care about or have commitments with.

Self-Sacrificing or over giving is often subconsciously tied to being liked. And keeping the peace. If over used in life it can cause stress reactions of martyrdom, resentment and even self-disparagement.

Taking RESPONSE-ability for your own needs is important to a satisfying, fulfilling life. It means that your happiness and welfare are just as important as everyone else's and should be prioritized.

YOU MATTER and you know it.
Give yourself permission to live that way, prioritizing yourself first.
Not only for you but also those watching you.
No one wants you to suffer, that's your choice.

Your Life By Design

Your Life By Design

_____

_____

_____

_____

_____

_____

_____

_____

_____

_____

_____

_____

_____

_____

_____

_____

_____

_____

_____

_____

_____

_____

_____

JOURNAL PROMPT

Remember, self-care is not selfish it is strategic.

When you take care of you, you feel better. AND, simultaneously, you are actually role modeling - giving others a real life example - of what self-care looks like.

Self-care fills your cup so you can better serve yourself and others. It is the foundation of a **life by design**. What does self-care currently look like for you?

As a leader, a member of a family, a friend group... you likely have many commitments. How strategic can you be with your own self-care routine in order to meet those commitments without resentment, burnout or frustration? Reflect on where and when you are prioritizing your own physical and mental health and overall well-being? Or perhaps, where you are not.

It's time.

JOURNAL PROMPT

EASE OR DIS-EASE

What if you stopped waiting for things to change?

What if you stopped blaming yourself for not knowing the answers?

What if you stopped lying to yourself about how satisfied you are?

What if you simply stopped ignoring your body and its needs?

What if you stopped avoiding negative or bad feelings and emotions?

What if you stopped saying no when you really want to say yes?

What if you stopped putting off your dreams, wants, & desires?

What if you stopped blaming others for your own dissatisfaction?

What if you actually stopped arguing for your limitations?

What if stopping made your life easier?

There is risk in resisting change.
What we resist persists.
The more you resist, avoid the present moment, ignore your needs and your heart's deepest desires, abuse yourself, blame others or avoid your emotional messaging system, the greater risk of **DIS- EASE**...disease.

What would the path of least resistance feel like?
Look like? Be like?
EASE-ier?
Only you know the answer.
And your body may already be telling you.

Your Life By Design

Nurturing Your Mind

Taking care of your **mind**, and the **words** and **images** you fill it with, is an essential aspect of self-care. It equates to your overall mental health and powers your well-being. **Emotional neglect** can lead to a range of issues, including **anxiety** and **depression** and ultimately prevent you from getting what you want out of life. Nurturing your way of **thinking and visualizing** in your mind's eye requires conscious thought and practice. Intentionally engaging in activities that promote mental wellness, such as **mindfulness, meditation, coaching and therapy** can enable you to create your ideal current reality. A **life by design** you love.

Mindfulness involves being present in the moment and paying attention to your thoughts and feelings with a hat of **curiosity**. Become the **observer** of yourself. That is all you need to powerfully create your life! Then practice with activities like yoga or breath-work.

Mirror work is also one of my favorite practices (*see Louise Hay's work*). Activities like these can help you to become more aware, more conscious, more powerful.

The goal? Become a creator of your life with a foundation of self-love, feelings of calm, intentional consciousness, and compassion.

Meditation is another favorite way of mine to nurture the mind. It involves focusing on a particular object or thought to quiet the mind and with practice is proven to reduce stress and create space for you to be in a state of choice, responding vs. reacting to your life. There are various types of meditation, including sitting, walking, silent or guided, mantra driven, and body scan meditations. You choose! Consider exploring meditation without expectation other than to try it out!

Are you willing to try? Do you need help?

Life By Design Journal

Nurturing Your Mind

Consider This:

Coaching + Therapy = A Life By Design.

Coaching, counseling and therapeutic support are essential resources for nurturing our mind, body, and soul connection strategically. AND, it is nothing to be ashamed of. Talking to a therapist can help you process your thoughts and emotions and develop sound, proven coping strategies for challenging situations. Partnering with a coach can help you clarify your values and goals and provide the clarity, sounding board, and accountability practices to propel you into your desired future state. Therapists and coaches ultimately provide **a safe space** for you to express your feelings and concerns, without judgement to
help you help yourself live your best life.

_____

_____

_____

_____

_____

_____

_____

_____

_____

_____

_____

JOURNAL PROMPT

Today, even if it's just for a moment or two, I want you to realize how remarkable you really are! Remarkable : Worthy of Attention! Striking!

Think about what you have overcome in your life: All the challenges, the heartbreaks, the loss, the fears.
Truly Remarkable!

Think about what you have accomplished so far: The impact you have made upon the world through the way you showed up every day, through the way you used your talents, through the support you gave to others, through the love you shared. You did that!
Truly Remarkable!

You are so unique. And we're so lucky you're here in this world. Receive that. Believe that. Embrace that. Know like you know like you know you are REMARKABLE. 🙌

Now, what REMARKS would you like to capture about yourself today?

JOURNAL PROMPT

Are you critical and judgmental about what's not going well? Notice if you're feeling victim to what is. Notice if 'what is' is getting in the way of what could be.

As a leader - and I mean a leader of self, of others, as a parent or family member, focusing too heavily on 'what is' can be the worse thing you could do if you want something different.

Your job as a leader, of self and others, is to hold the vision of what could be. The dream of what can be! You must define it so you can design it.

OPPORTUNITIES-POSSIBILITIES-VISIONS-SOLUTIONS

Lead the way for those you lead, especially yourself!
Don't judge, criticize, play the victim to your situation, your finances, your time, your lack of resources, your circumstances... enough already.
All of that = wasted time.

Instead, be curious, assess the facts, keep the faith & SIMPLY LEAD. Sure it can be a challenge sometimes, but this is what you signed up for, isn't it?! This is why you said yes to these many roles in your life. Are you not at choice? (If you aren't, definitely journal about THAT).

Miracles can happen when you're focused on the things that matter most to you. Remember, where the mind goes energy flows AND expands! It's your job to embody and role model that in your life. How willing are you?

Your Life By Design

Nourishing Your Body

Taking care of your body is a crucial aspect of self-care, self-love. **Our bodies** are the vessels that carry us through life, and we know that neglecting them can lead to a range of health and emotional issues. Believe me, I definitely know. I struggled with an eating disorder in my late teens and early twenties and naturally that experience has had a significant influence on my own self-care, self-love journey.

Sometimes it is positive, often negative and now mostly neutral.

I overcame it by doing this type of self-coaching work until I accepted and healed the part of me that didn't feel enough and felt out of control.

You can see now that nourishing your body involves more than physical wellness, such as exercise, healthy eating, and getting enough rest.

It actually requires a foundation of undeniable self-worth, feeling enough, and learning to intentionally focus on your why and your deservedness.

Having this knowing makes it a lot easier to choose to **move your body**!

Exercise, or as I prefer to call it movement (*check out The Anti Fitness Movement blog by Dominique Geary, who is also a guest on Coffee With Nicoa S1 Ep16*), is one of the most effective ways to nourish our bodies and improve our well-being and life longevity. Really **listen to your body**. It already knows what it needs.

Start **asking your body**, how do you like to move?

I personally like dancing in the kitchen, doing pushups against the bathroom counter, and stretching in the bed! Sometimes I spin in the yard, practice squatting down and standing up without my hands and I even do wall sits while I wait for my coffee to be made! Really! Is that all exercise?

You better believe it is!

And if it is fun for me, I am more likely to do it.

Nourishing Your Body

I treat eating similarly to moving my body.

I intuitively eat what I crave, what I need, asking my body what it craves and what it needs. **WITHOUT JUDGEMENT!** You know, food doesn't have morality. It isn't good or bad. And calories are needed to fuel and energize your body.

You need calories!

Nutrition is about finding the nutrients that your body needs to exist! Without proper nutrients we can not live, and we are not our best selves. **The selves the world needs!**

Getting enough **SLEEP** is another critical aspect of self-care. **Rest** is essential for our physical and mental health, and neglecting it can lead to a range of health issues. Did you know adults typically need to get at least seven hours of sleep each night? Developing good sleep habits, such as sticking to a regular sleep schedule, avoiding caffeine late in the day and blue light electronics before bed, along with creating a relaxing sleep environment, can help.

I also highly recommend naps!

What else could you try?

Regular massage, acupuncture, energy work, chiropractic.

Remember, it's your one and only body. **How will you nourish it?**

_____

_____

_____

_____

_____

_____

_____

_____

_____

_____

JOURNAL PROMPT

Your body knows what to do.

Think about how you think about food. Do you judge it as good or bad? Do you judge your body as good or bad? Your body is a whole system connected to your mind through your intuition, your soulful knowing.

Your body knows when it's hungry, needs rest, when it needs to stretch and move and if you listen carefully it will send you messages with aches, pains, and intuitive thoughts that say "Hello... I need something from you."

What is your current relationship with your body?

Your body is smarter than you think it is.
Pause and think about that for a moment. Your body already knows what to do. You don't even have to tell it to function, right?
It just keeps going! Unless you aren't listening to it.
Your only job is to listen to it and respond with
TLC: tender love and care!

The misconception is that we are somehow in control of our bodies. "If this, then that" thinking. Yes, I understand that certain behaviors do have outcomes that may not be the healthiest. But, what if I told you that you may be doing too much to TRY to influence your body and you're actually confusing it.

Get to know your body as a PARTNER to your soul, instead of a PART of you that you need to control. This releases the resistance to 'what is' in order to integrate and allow what naturally will be -- the perfection that is your body.

What does your body need?

Your Life By Design

JOURNAL PROMPT

When was the last time you paused and took a big deep breath? Do it with me now.

Just breathe in and breathe out.
Notice the sensations in your body as you practice. Notice the presence it creates for you. Notice where your mind goes.

Literally breath gives us life. We must have it to nourish our bodies to survive.
You can always come back to your breath.

What if you took breathing to another level? Welcome in the concept of Breath-work.

People have been practicing breath-work for thousands of years, and it has roots in the practice of yoga. The basic idea of breath-work is to nourish your mind and body when you breathe in and release toxins and stress when you breathe out.

The Relaxing Breath from Andrew Weil, M.D., also known as 4-7-8 breathing, helps to slow down and calm the body.

It slows the heart rate, brings our consciousness to the present moment, and slows the nervous system, bringing a feeling of calm and peace.

This breathing technique is ideal when you are feeling overwhelmed, anxious, angry, triggered, or having trouble sleeping. Try it now: Empty your lungs of air, breathe in through your nose for 4 seconds, hold your breath for 7 seconds, exhale out of the mouth for 8 seconds, and repeat at least 4 times.
This practice creates space in the body, bringing you into the present releasing excess energy and thought from the mind.

Repeat and Reflect.

JOURNAL PROMPT

Sleep is the best meditation. - Dalai Lama

Did you know that you spend about 1/3 of your life asleep?!
Yes, literally sleeping.

Sleep is a state of reduced mental and physical activity in which consciousness is altered and sensory activity is inhibited to a certain extent. It allows your brain and body to rest. And, I would add, it gives your soul the necessary time to reflect, restore, and rejuvenate so you can take on another day!

We all know that if we do not get enough sleep, our body and our mind suffer as a result.
The basic tips for better sleep are pretty obvious - regular time to bed, no caffeine late in the day, using the bed for sleep AND sex (wink, wink) and typically not for tv, work or other activities, etc. etc. etc.

Let's talk, however, about your emotional relationship with sleep. How well do you sleep?
What are you making sleep, or not sleeping, mean to you?
Do you like sleep? Is sleep an achilles heel for you? Do you judge sleep as good or bad? Are naps fulfilling or considered laziness?
What happens when you can't sleep...
what are your actual thoughts?

Sleep is underrated if you ask me.
You deserve to sleep. You body knows how to sleep. So, if you are not sleeping well, barring any known medical, medication or substance interference reasons, try asking your body why it is not sleeping well. Listen. Perhaps reflect on whether there is something subconsciously telling you it isn't safe to sleep.
Be curious.

JOURNAL PROMPT

What are the top three secrets to a fulfilling life by design?

Your Body. Your Emotions. Your Language.

Wondering whether a choice is wise or not? Don't default search your mind for a rational argument. Try holding each option in your attention, then feel its effect on your **body**, on your **emotions**. Notice your **language**, too. What story are you telling about this choice? When something's wrong for you, you'll likely feel constriction or tightness rooted in a stress reaction or negative feeling. Yet, the wise choice leads to feelings of liberation, freedom, ease. It is your story that helps you shift your perception to better align to a wiser path.

You might notice if the root of any anxiety you experience is coming from the meaning you are giving the situation filtered by your own doubts, uncertainties or fears. What are your words telling the world and you about this situation? Are those words based in FEAR or LOVE?

Do you have a fear of being judged or rejected? You may say "But wait, I'm not afraid of what others think - I am afraid of failure or getting it wrong." Okay, that's normal. Ask yourself what drives that fear? Root cause practice, ask yourself WHY 5X, dig deep and see what answer you receive.

See how we reflected there? Root cause analysis takes practice and listening to your body, validating your emotions, and noticing your language. Practice finding the ease in your body and your mind & emotions will inevitably follow.
Then you can choose wisely.

Your Life By Design

Tending to Your SOUL

When you do things from your soul, you feel a river moving in you, a joy.
-Rumi

Dr. Shelley Harrel's research shows us that as a collective, we believe our SOUL is some or all facets of the following:

An experience of depth, a deeply felt sensing; Authenticity and "realness"; A source of truth, wisdom, and knowing; A sense of aliveness, an inner liberation, being "moved" from within; A source of strength and resilience; An inner resource for healing and refuge; A source of inspiration; A reminder of our own humanity and our connection to the humanity of others; A profound sense of resonance and connection with shared lived experience; An experience of our transcendent interconnectedness with humanity, nature, spirit; Our deepest core where our humanness and spirit meet.

How aware and connected are you to your soul? What in the above resonates most with your experience of your soul?

Dr. Harrel invites us to ponder the idea that tending to your soul can be an unshackling and unchaining, breaking free from what holds you back, holds you down, or imprisons you. It is about observing and seeing what we are chained to and entangled with so that we can be clear that we are more than our conditions or circumstances, know the truth of our own worth, connect to ancestral wisdom and the cultural strength deep within us, and access that internal energy to participate in the liberation of our bodies, minds, hearts, and souls.

For me, my soul is the essence of me. The part of me that wants to experience all of the feels, all of the emotions, and all sensory experiences my body can offer me. I want this for everyone so much so that I do my absolute best to embody this way of Being for all to see and learn from. I want to show you that you, too, can live in a state of Being that is steeped in unlimited possibilities!

Soulful Living is Mindful Living

Tending to your **soul** is an essential aspect of **strategic self-care**. Your soul, spirit, higher self - whatever you choose to call it, is essentially the essence of who you are, and neglecting it always leads to a sense of disconnection and unease.

Feeling lonely? Maybe you aren't listening to that inner voice and inner knowing. That's your soul talking. Sometimes it's hard to hear. Self-care practices that tend to your soul involve **fostering space to hear that inner voice** and impact your overall spiritual wellness. It can be as simple as practicing daily gratitude, spending time in nature, being playful, or pursuing creative endeavors,

How often do you participate in any of these examples in your life?
The idea is that when you practice these types of activities it can open you up energetically and remind you to listen to and learn to follow your intuition. The more you listen and allow yourself to act on your intuition the more self-trust you uncover. Self-trust to know you are safe to listen to that inner guidance. It is your truth. Don't worry, you'll remember how.

Let's begin with Gratitude. Do you intentionally practice gratitude?
Focusing on the **positive aspects of your life** and expressing **gratitude** helps to cultivate peace, contentment, and overall optimism. Journaling about what you love in your life really helps (*ding, ding, ding, that's what you're doing!*).
Research shows that by making a gratitude list in your mind or on paper literally rewires your brain for positivity and raises your vibration so that you actually attract **MORE** to be grateful for! *Like energy attracts like energy* - it's physics!

Pause and reflect on what you DO love about a person? What ARE you grateful for about your job? What IS beautiful about this rainy day? Why do you love washing those dishes? How does cleaning your house make your life even better? Even paying a bill can be rooted in gratitude!!

You own connecting the dots of **gratitude** to what matters most to you. The question is how willing are you to put your attention to those things you're truly grateful for?

Soulful Living is Mindful Living

Spending time in **nature** is another way to tend to your soul. Convening with nature even if you're looking at a photograph of a beautiful outdoor scene, has a way of soothing **our minds and our spirits** and can help us to feel more **connected to the world** around us. I remember when I would get stressed at work and would call my Mom to vent and complain. She would always say to me, *"Nicoa, go find a window and look outside at the trees! Can you do that now?"* she'd encourage. It always helped. Activities like sky gazing, forest bathing, hiking, camping, going barefoot in the grass or simply spending any time outside that you can create for yourself can help you to feel more grounded and at peace, able to see the world with **fresh eyes** again.

Go walk around outside of the house or office, right now! I dare you.
(don't worry, this can wait, it'll be here when you get back!)

Your soul is also constantly craving ways to be **creative**, too.
Are you answering that creativity call deep down inside?
I recently bought tap shoes and took a tap class. Hey, why not? It was **fun**! Creativity is available to us in so many ways, as an extra curricular activity, hobbies or even in our work. Whatever your creative endeavors are they fuel your connection with your soul and increase your access to long lasting happiness. Pursuing activities like designing something, painting, writing, or playing music, can help you express yourself in new and meaningful ways. Maybe it is making Reels on Instagram or TikTok that **lights you up**! Notice too, that these types of activities can help you process emotions and find new perspectives on challenging situations. There are so many benefits to taking that break and fostering your creativity! I have noticed the more creative breaks I take and the more fun I foster, the more ideas I get to help grow and expand my own **life by design**!

What does light you up?
How does that resonate with YOUR soul?

JOURNAL PROMPT

A sense of real leisure, a feeling of freedom, exemption, free from duty, immunity earned by service...These are the words associated with "VACATION". Vacation allows us to "be empty, at leisure, to leave, abandon. From the Latin word "vacare," it means to be unoccupied.

Sitting alone with one's thoughts? Being Mindful? Perhaps being so present you are unattached to any particular outcomes? Going with the flow?

PAUSE and REFLECT on your own VACATIONING

How easy is it for you to be unoccupied?
Do you prefer to vacation solo, with friends or family, or with a group of strangers? Why?
What is the best vacation you've ever taken?
What made it the best?
What have you learned about yourself on vacations?
What is the next vacation you'd love to take?
Or maybe you are on vacation at this very moment!
If you are, how does it feel to be you right now?
Do you find ease or challenge in vacationing?

Being the observer of you and your current mood, your emotions, your story, your way of being gives you the power to intentionally create whatever vacation you desire.

What type of vacation experience do you desire? What would be your ideal way of Being on vacation?

JOURNAL PROMPT

That was your intuition guiding you toward the path of least resistance!

Just notice.
Accepting your own internal guidance usually feels like a real relief even if you're debating or second guessing a tough life situation. Not accepting the situation as is, is resistance.
Are you negatively thinking about "it"?
If anxiety or angst appear, that is likely resistance at play.

Be still. Listen. The truth is a release, easier, peaceful, loving, generous, forgiving feeling. YOUR TRUTH is a guiding force always pointing you towards your TRUE NORTH.
Breathe. release and, for just a moment, surrender into this awareness.
What does your gut tell you?
Does it feel good?

Consider these thoughts

"I choose to let go."
"I am open to an easier solution."
"I trust an easier solution will present itself"
"My feelings are valid yet I trust there's an easier way."
"May this solution be in the best interest for all involved."

Releasing mental control by relaxing your body and allowing solutions to present themselves to you through your inner voice - your gut - your truth - your intuition - THIS my friend is a powerful self-care life skill. Just ask yourself, your higher self, to listen and present you with your truth.
And if that is tricky and difficult, just go back to the beginning of this prompt and start again.
It's a practice. Choose a situation you're facing today. Place your hand on your heart and listen for guidance. What do you hear? If emotions come up, sit with them. That's the message.

Your Life By Design

Your Life By Design

_____

_____

_____

_____

_____

_____

_____

_____

_____

_____

_____

_____

_____

_____

_____

_____

_____

_____

_____

_____

_____

_____

Your Life By Design

JOURNAL PROMPT

I read somewhere that boldness is more of an indicator of success than intelligence. I believe this. I mean, heck, I became a top HR executive and didn't even have a degree in HR! If I hadn't been bold enough to ask to be considered for an HR job that I really wanted early on in my career...well, who knows where my path would have taken me.

People who are **BOLD** in their pursuit of their goals and what they want tend to think more about what is possible and what will go well in their lives. They believe in their ability to learn and "figure it out" by leveraging their resources. Asking. Being a bold thinker is based on trusting yourself and anticipating life working out for you.

On the other hand, the opposite of bold is **timid**. People who are timid may over think, ruminate about worse case scenarios and get stuck too long in the "yes, buts" and the "why bother" mindset. They have a tendency to hesitate, coming from a space of scarcity, fear and uncertainty and may not take action at all.

So what?

BOLDNESS changes, disrupts, grows, solves, creates, and expands your world.
While TIMIDNESS does <u>none</u> of those things.

Where would being **BOLD** serve your life by design for the better today?

Creating Self-Care Rituals

Creating self-care **rituals** in your **life by design** can be an essential aspect of prioritizing **your own needs** and making your overall well-being sacred. An intentional self-care ritual is yours and yours alone helping you manage stress, feel loved, improve your physical health, and continue to foster **YOUR** definition of good mental health. Yes, this is all yours and worth creating! A key first step in creating an intentional self-care ritual is to identify the activities that bring you joy and help you to feel grounded.

When was the last time you felt that way?
What brings you consistency and contentment?

Exploring different areas of your life and experimenting with what works best for you can be fun and exciting. Choose for it to be fun and exciting! Maybe your daily face washing routine? When you take your shower? Walking the dog? Making your coffee? Sitting under your favorite tree or in your favorite chair? Or something else?

I love driving on my favorite roads in town, even though they aren't always the fastest way! Washing my face every night and savoring the luxury of nourishing my skin with beautiful cleansers, creams and oils helps me feel well-cared for and gives me a boost of self-love. Making my coffee every morning - deciding which cup I will use, steaming or frothing the creamer, and overall savoring each sip while sitting in bed with my husband is an intentional self-care ritual for me, and him.

Oh and **journaling daily**, too!

Meditating whenever I feel like it is also powerful (*I love using my Monroe Institute App*), or just listening to my favorite music, at FULL BLAST! I even intentionally use my favorite pens throughout the day! Definitely eating nutritious foods that energize me is a plus. Saying no to alcohol when I don't want to imbibe even though others around me are choosing to drink.

These are **ALL** rituals and practices that serve my **life by design**.

What comes to mind for YOU?

Once you have identified the many **self-care rituals** that work best for you, it is important to make them a regular part of your **life by design**. Don't freak out, I don't mean you have to commit to a daily routine, unless you really want to. This may involve setting aside specific times each day or finding ways to incorporate them into your existing routines. But in general, be **flexible** and have **fun** moving in and out of what makes you **happy** each day. It's all about you, what makes **YOU** feel good.

This is YOUR life by design.

It may also be motivating to track your progress and celebrate your successes along the way. **Use this journal** to track your progress, **celebrate** the emotional fulfillment of sticking to your rituals and reflecting often on your **beautiful experiences** by writing them down or sharing them on social media or with a close friend. They are yours. Hold them sacred because remember, **you are always the priority** when it comes to strategic self-care.

This process and journey is a fresh opportunity to give yourself **permission to prioritize** your own needs and find ways to cultivate a sense of balance and fulfillment in your life. By **exploring** different self-care rituals and really making them a regular part of your life, you will foster and promote a greater sense of well-being and lead a happier, healthier, sustainable **life by design**.

You Deserve It!

JOURNAL PROMPT

Look at all you've accomplished in just the past week! Not to mention the past six months, and year and oh right...can you believe how time flies?!? LOOK AT THE PAST DECADE!

Today try on the energy of Oneness where joy, peace and connection are all about savoring the outcomes of the journey.
The journey is all about YOU!
YOU did that. YOU did this. YOU'RE doing it ALL!
You're designing your life!

Consider that we are all connected. Oneness meaning that what I see in you, is also in me. You, therefore, designing your life impacts me designing mine. If you did something, then I did something. The joy of the Olympic athlete winning the gold medal is felt as strongly as the the individual drowning across the globe from a tsunami.

We are one.
I am you.
And you are me.
What if you choose to see everyone through this reality?

Today I invite us both to celebrate the collective consciousness that is WE!

Strategic Self-Care for Difficult Times

Strategic self-care practices can vary depending on the situation. Context and circumstance often dictate what is possible day in and day out for each of us. Keeping in mind your goal of peace, calm, satisfaction and ... *you finish filling in this list* ... it is absolutely possible to become part of your **way of Being** to naturally remember your practices and rituals to off set situational challenges.
Call them coping mechanisms?
Or perhaps, my favorite phrase, **life by design** practices?

Let's talk about the difficult times. There are specific practices that can be helpful during times of stress, illness, or grief as some key examples. Understanding the different types of self-care practices and trusting when to use them can help you to **take care of yourself** with greater ease during challenging times.

During times of stress, like the above shared examples, I invite you back to two basic life by design foundational practices:

Self-awareness and listening to your inner voice.
Begin by asking yourself what you need - like deep breathing
(*see the breath-work prompt*), basic self-care like a shower, maybe stillness of a meditation or getting outside in nature...or maybe some gentle body movement like stretching? All of which, as we know, can be super helpful in bringing your body and mind back to center. Remember that you can do hard things, you are strong, and you have phenomenal coping mechanisms to handle difficult times. By observing yourself and listening to that inner voice, you'll always know what you, and your body, mind and soul need to feel better.

This is your life by design.

After instilling rituals and practices into your life, over time, you'll learn to **trust** yourself to know what you need. And **listening** to that **inner knowing**, your **intuition**, begins to override stress reactions and unhealthy behaviors that no longer serve you. Only you know if reading or taking a bath or eating a bag of chips or binge watching a Netflix show is what is strategic self-care for you. That's where you begin.

What do you want? And how is what you are doing getting you what you want? Finding **compassion** and giving yourself **permission** moment to moment to do what you want and need, well, that is a choice and it is yours and yours alone. The moment that choice no longer serves you will also be presented to your **inner knowing** and then you may, or may not, decide to choose differently.

We all know that activities like getting enough sleep, eating healthy foods, and staying hydrated can help our bodies to heal and recover, too. So don't discount these **basic primary needs**. Start there if you are unsure what you need. And of course, during times of grief, it is essential to prioritize **self-compassion and connection** with others to stay on track to healing. Please seek support from a therapist or support group if you are struggling. **Whatever you are experiencing is normal.** Trust that you know what you need. Trust yourself to align those needs with what matters most to you.

Finding ways to achieve **a moment of solace** as you recover from whatever stressor life has handed you is always your number one **priority**! You should now have your own growing go-to list of strategic self-care rituals to help you do just that. Yes, I know it can be tough. BUT, here's another reminder of the beauty in this process of overcoming challenging situations...**YOU always get to decide** what brings you that relief. And you decide whether it serves you for the short term or for the long term. Do this without any judgment. The key is to remember to do them.

JOURNAL PROMPT

Fear is a natural reaction to moving closer to the truth. - Pema Chodron

Ever worry you are making the wrong choice? What if that fear you have about deciding which direction to take is telling you something even greater?

The fact you may worry about a decision may simply be your emotions asking you to look closer at what matters most to you, or reminding you that you may be out of balance and need to ground yourself before proceeding. What is fear telling you? Is there truth in this message?

Accepting that there is no wrong choice can provide you with some relief when fear shows up, yes? Sure there may be a painful lesson as a result but the state of indecision driven by fear may be a much heavier load to bear in life than choosing to choose.
What is the cost of not making a decision? What is the benefit of deciding?

Fear often shows up as anxiety and anxiety is a close cousin to excitement. The body reacts in very similar ways in both emotions. One is steeped in worry about a future that may not work out as one wishes and the other is based on anticipation that the future works out exactly as hoped!

Or something even better...

Your Life By Design

JOURNAL PROMPT

Don't resist what 'IS' any longer.

You can not control situations and outcomes that have already occurred but you can control your perception of them. If you suffer over what 'IS' then you are in a state of resistance. This is important to ponder. What would acceptance of what 'IS' look and feel like to you?

Acceptance is allowing the present moment to be as it is without judgement.
Mindfulness.
Being here now.
In complete acceptance and presence you may recognize a clarity of thinking where you are at 100% choice.

When you are at choice you can then move down the path of least resistance so as to reduce your own suffering. It doesn't mean you stay where you are and just give in or give up - far from it - it means you move toward what you want with greater ease. And if like energy attracts like energy, then that energetic approach of acceptance will create a way of being that attracts more ease and solutions toward your "something even better!" outcome.

Should. Have to. Need to. Want to. Choose to.
Where are you most often?
What is getting between you and acceptance?

Your Life By Design

_____

_____

_____

_____

_____

_____

_____

_____

_____

_____

_____

_____

_____

_____

_____

_____

_____

_____

_____

_____

_____

_____

_____

Overcoming Barriers to Self-Care

While creating a strategic self-care routine is important for promoting overall well-being, it is not always easy as you know. Many of us face various barriers that can make it difficult to prioritize our own needs and engage in self-care activities and this journal does't want to discount that fact. I think about privilege and circumstance frequently. Yet, I still believe we can find presence and awareness that fosters self-care even in the most dire of circumstances.

Today let's reflect on some of the most common ones:

Time constraints: Many of us lead busy lives and may struggle to find time for self-care activities. I ask you to focus on your perception of time. Are you a victim to it or do you see unlimited possibilities? What story are you telling? Start small and see if you can find the time, make the time, design the time!

Guilt or shame: Some individuals may feel guilty or ashamed for taking time for themselves, particularly if they feel like they should be focusing on their responsibilities or taking care of others. Where does this guilt and shame stem from? Doing the work on understanding your tendencies toward these emotions could be life changing to enable you to let them go and release the resulting self-abuse they have created for you. It's your life and your story and you can't get it wrong. If you find yourself feeling guilty or ashamed for taking time for yourself, challenge these negative thoughts by reminding yourself that self-care is strategic and important to you for your overall well-being. Repeat!

Lack of support: Some individuals may not have access to support from friends or loved ones, which can make it difficult to engage in self-care activities. Can you find support elsewhere? Do you need help or do you need to simply let something go, or both? What would help look like for you? Sometimes we prefer to sit in a "no one helps me" story because we are in some way benefitting from gaining the sympathy or attention that overwhelm creates. Something to ponder.

Financial constraints: Some self-care activities may be expensive or require resources that individuals may not have access to but most are free. Sitting still for 5 minutes breathing. Nature. A hug. A conversation. Watching a funny show. Taking a bath. Washing your face. Rearranging your room. Washing your sheets and making your bed. Saying no to something you'd rather not do.

See what I mean?

Mental health challenges: Individuals who are struggling with mental health challenges may find it difficult to engage in self-care activities, particularly if they are experiencing symptoms like fatigue, lack of motivation, or difficulty concentrating. Try observing your thoughts and remind yourself that you are the creator of those thoughts. You own your self-talk. What would you prefer to think, feel, say to yourself about today, this moment, self-care. Of course, if you don't have support from friends or loved ones, please do ask for help, seek support, dial 988 (or your country's mental health hotline) if you feel despair.

Remember, you are loved and deserve self-love.

This understanding is the foundation required to overcome barriers - knowing you are loved and lovable and deserve to treat yourself well in order to live your best life! Overcoming barriers to self-care requires a **willingness** to prioritize your own needs and find creative solutions to the challenges you face. By taking small steps and seeking support when needed, you can overcome these obstacles and make self-care a regular part of your strategic **life by design** routine.

How willing are you?

JOURNAL PROMPT

Ever spent hours on end replaying a scene or interaction from your day that you wish had gone differently? Maybe you made a mistake or showed up in a way that you wish you hadn't?

Rumination can ruin an evening.

But remember:

That's totally normal.
You're human.
Not a bad person.
Not broken.
Just doing the best you can.

Let it go.
The past is over.

Come back into the present moment and savor what is right in front of you.

Oh, and tomorrow? It's a brand new day!

Try treating each day like a clean sheet of paper and write your story anew from there.
Where would you like to restart with a clean sheet of paper today?
Rumination be damned!

Your Life By Design

_____

_____

_____

_____

_____

_____

_____

_____

_____

_____

_____

_____

_____

_____

_____

_____

_____

_____

_____

_____

Your Life By Design

_____

_____

_____

_____

_____

_____

_____

_____

_____

_____

_____

_____

_____

_____

_____

_____

_____

_____

_____

_____

_____

_____

_____

JOURNAL PROMPT

Notice if you default to seeing the world through a lense of negativity more often than not.
Do you tend to always look for how things aren't working or might not work out,
more so than what is working out?

The alternative ... practice considering the possibilities & opportunities that are being created within the same situation? What's another way to look at it? How does shifting your view make you feel?

Now, don't blame yourself or beat yourself up—this is just how humans are wired. So normal! Our survival instincts constantly leave us waiting for whatever proverbial sh*t is about to hit the fan.

But you are an evolved human being who has a conscious choice!
Today why not consider the following questions:

How can this situation open up a new opportunity?

What might be a way this could work out well?

What are three or more beneficial options that this situation presents me with?

Or simply ask yourself: What's possible here?

Your Life By Design

JOURNAL PROMPT

Don't wait for the perfect moment.
Take the moment and make it perfect.

Where can you practice acceptance without the need to judge critically, but just observe curiously?

Where can you question another's behavior without reacting or resisting it?

Where can you allow the chaos to just be a set of facts and then consciously choose to respond based on what matters most in that moment?

What would you really like to do next?
You own this thing called life, now live it!

Pay attention, your negative thoughts only beget more of the same...releasing and allowing what is to "just be" and then choosing what you wish to do next is a practice worth trying. And actually doing it! Living!

I want to share a scene from one of my favorite movies called "**AUNTIE MAME**" that I believe sums up this point:

Mame Dennis : "Oh, Agnes, where is your spine? Here you've been taking my dictation for weeks and you don't get the message of my book. Live, that's the message!"

Agnes Gooch: Live?

Mame Dennis: Yes! Life is a banquet and most poor suckers are starving to death! (*except she doesn't say poor suckers! LOL*)

Your Life By Design

Self-Care and Well-Being

Your overall **well-being** and **mental health** are intrinsically connected to the practice of self-care and should not be forgotten. Let's delve into that intricate relationship explaining how the two are intertwined and how you can leverage self-care to foster better mental health and wellness. I've referenced the power of the mind and the body earlier in this journal, so keep those concepts in the forefront as you read on.

Our minds and bodies are not separate entities; they function in **tandem, integrated, partnering.** We know that mental health issues can cause physical ailments and vice versa - I truly believe, and so does the research of Louise Hay, that every illness and element of **"DIS - EASE"** comes from an energetic set of beliefs being processed through our internal physical systems messaging us of a need for attention. Self-care, from a holistic standpoint, can influence all aspects of the body and mind, acting as a bridge that supports and enhances your mental health. Full stop.

You've already been reminded that **stress reduction** can be significantly influenced by breath-work, meditation, moving your body, fueling your body, etc. all of which have been proven to **reduce cortisol levels** (a stress hormone) in the body. Adopting these practices not only makes us feel more relaxed and at ease but most importantly aids our **cognitive functioning and mood regulation.** Simply making you feel better!

Endorphin-releasing activities, like exercise, laughter, and even socializing, can act as natural mood lifters. Keeping these facts in mind gives you **power**, gives you **choice**, gives you the **solution** to your overwhelm in most cases! Let's look at some foundational practices and options available to you.

A critical element of all of this work is beginning with **observation of self, or Self-awareness**. It is the foundation of this journal actually. Research has proven that by Journaling, practicing reflection and intentional introspection, or self-awareness, we become more mindful and more conscious of our choices. And Mindfulness undeniably helps you understand your state of mind and your emotions, making it easier to address negative thought patterns and see a way forward to what you want in life. Once you harness this practice of self observation you can begin to see the interplay of strategic self-care and your mental health and well-being.

Setting Boundaries as self-care is a critical practice to learn. Boundaries, both physical and emotional, are vital for mental well-being. They ensure we don't overextend ourselves, safeguarding us from burnout and emotional fatigue. Pause for a moment and ask yourself, what boundary for you is not being set? How are you giving away your energy by not speaking up or sharing what you want and need in your life? Are you doing more for others in order to be loved or liked at a cost to your own mental health?

The role of professional help should be considered. While self-care is a powerful tool in maintaining mental well-being, it's essential to recognize when professional help may be needed. Do you have someone to talk to, someone you can share with that isn't personally invested in you? Someone that isn't your partner, your family member or even your best friend? Therapists, counselors and coaches can offer safe, third party professional guidance, resources, and strategies tailored to your individual needs. There is no shame in seeking professional help.

All in all, the symbiotic relationship between self-care and your mental well-being is undeniable. By understanding this interlink, you can harness the power of self-care to significantly enhance your life...FOREVER! The struggle is real, yes, but you are not alone and you don't have to be if you remember you can ask for help. It's an ongoing journey for sure, one where consistent effort and **self-awareness** can lead to a **balanced, healthy mind** and **life by design** you **love**.

JOURNAL PROMPT

Have you ever really noticed the power of your energy and how it brings to you similar energy from others? And the opposite is true, too, right? We mirror each other.

So let's be intentional, shall we?!
Stop and take a deep breath. Okay, do that again, like, really take a deep breath.

Step #1:
Ask yourself "What do I want to attract today?
Love? Excitement? Creativity? Opportunities?
Open Mindedness?
Hope? Passion?

Step #2:
Become the energy that you want to attract.
BE love. BE excited. BE creative. BE opportunistic.
BE open minded.
BE hope. BE passion.

You are an energetic human BEING,
not a human DOING.
Ahhhhh, that feels better, yes? How else do you want to shift your way of Being today?

JOURNAL PROMPT

You are the vibrational writer of the script of your life, and everyone else in the Universe is playing the part that you have assigned to them.

Life by Design. Energy Leadership. Thoughts. Emotions. Behavior. You are the creator of your life!

> But Nicoa...
> If 'you know who' would just do what I need them to do!
> If it weren't for 'so - n - so' things would be different!
> 'They' sure do get my goat, ya know!!??
> Ugh I really dislike that person!
> If it weren't for them I could create my life better!

> Which assumption are you living under when it comes to the people in your world? Either you believe they are showing up this way FOR you or against you.

I prefer FOR you! There's power in FOR you. There's victimhood in against you.

> Which assumption would you prefer to choose?

Your Life By Design

Your Life By Design

JOURNAL PROMPT

Remember when you pause and criticize someone and share that criticism with a colleague, a peer, an employee, even a friend or family member... all they may hear is how you are likely to criticize them with others behind their back.

> **Notice the potentially wasted mind share of using your time criticizing others. Not to mention the amount of time you may be criticizing yourself! How can you shift the need to criticize to a more fruitful discussion?**

Can you shift it to a diplomatic observation of another person's behavior and take the conversation into a state of problem solving? or curiosity?

Ask yourself, why does this bother me so much? Why am I talking about this person? Does this conversation improve my life? My circumstance?

Are you sharing to get advice or counsel? What if you spent that energy lifting someone up in reflection of what they do well in spite of their indiscretion or foible?

Maybe your frustration is the result of a missing conversation with the person? Or maybe your frustration is a reflection of your own self judgment?

> Remember, like energy attracts like energy. You get to choose. Yes, everyone is watching how you show up in this vain, but only you know what legacy you want to leave behind.
> Ask yourself,
> Is what I am about to say bringing value to the world? to me? to others? or is it a wasted breath?

Self-Care Rituals In Daily Life: How's It Going?

You're quite a ways through this journal. **Congratulations**! You probably realize more than ever now that **strategic self-care** activities can be so beneficial, and yet still can be difficult to fit into your busy life. Am I right? Pause for a moment to commend yourself for doing whatever you have been able to do so far, even if it is reading this page in this very moment. Right? **READING THIS PAGE** right now, for yourself is **AMAZING!**

I am so proud of you!

Woo Hoo! Now, let's keep it up! You deserve it!

Additional tips to reflect upon for incorporating self-care into your day:

Schedule it: Just like we schedule appointments and meetings, we can schedule self-care activities into our calendar. Whether it's a daily yoga practice or a weekly date with a friend, scheduling self-care activities can help us to prioritize them and make them a regular part of our routine. Heck, I even schedule taking a shower when I get busy!

Find small moments: Self-care doesn't always have to involve a big activity. Finding small moments throughout the day, such as taking a few deep breaths or stretching, can help us to feel grounded and refreshed. This counts! I like walking slowly to the mailbox and then sitting outside to open my mail.

Ahhhhh.

A brief respite from my calendar.

Create breaks to practice: Whether it's a lunch break or a quick 10-minute break of your own doing, use these moments to engage in self-care activities. This could involve going for a walk, practicing meditation, or simply taking a few deep breaths (*again with the breathing, right?*). I like to do other things, too, like practice juggling, playing with devil sticks (*so fun, look it up! they'd make a great gift - for YOU!*) or taking 5 min.'s to shoot hoops at the basketball goal! Oh, and of course, naps are good, too!

Let's keep going...

Find some friends: Self-care doesn't have to be a solitary activity. Find social activities, such as going for a walk with a friend or taking a yoga or dance class with a partner or, like me, hosting a party at my house or planning a brunch outing with friends. Plus, that's something to look forward to on my calendar which in and of itself is self-care for me!

Stay stocked up on self-care supplies: Whether it's this journal, a yoga mat, running shoes or a coloring book (*I like coloring with Ultra Fine Sharpie markers!*), keeping self-care supplies on hand can make it easier to engage in self-care activities when you have a free moment.
A client and I decided if she left her yoga mat unrolled behind her desk she was 80% more likely to pause and do some yoga between calls or even when she was just listening! It worked! And I do the same thing now.
I love a tried and true best practice!

Use your technology: There are many self-care apps available now that can help you practice mindfulness, and even track your progress, or suggest activities to keep you engaged and stay motivated. I love my Apple smart watch because I can schedule moments to pause, breathe or reflect pre-set to a timer and I also love seeing how many steps I get each day! It tracks those, too! Embracing technology can actually be a de-stressor!
It just depends on how you look at it.

Remember, these are just a few tips. This is YOUR Life By Design...you can design it any way you'd like...what else could you do?

_____

_____

_____

_____

_____

_____

_____

_____

JOURNAL PROMPT

Everything you experience is in response to your energetic viewpoint and vibration. Let's say it again, **like energy attracts like energy.**

Your vibration is offered out to your world because of what you are thinking, and you can tell by the way you feel, the emotions you are experiencing, by what kinds of thoughts you are having. That creates your vibe!
To shift out of something that's not serving you or is not making you feel good, you must find good-feeling thoughts immediately and as a result good-feeling manifestations must follow.
This is science.

LETS PRACTICE

Decide, right now, to look for the best-feeling aspects of whatever you are giving your attention to that has been a struggle for you recently...and if that seems unattainable just redirect your thoughts and look only for good-feeling things to give your attention to.

This is a conscious, intentional, deliberate
self-care practice:
Redirecting your attention OR
changing your perception of what you're attending to ...
that is the answer. You are the creator and the controller of your thoughts, remember? Start there.

Watch your life feel better, look better, get better as a result. Guaranteed! Practice this now as you journal.

JOURNAL PROMPT

As we are often asked to do in the working world, it's just as important to notice and reflect on what's not working well in our own world.

How so?
Instead of continually experiencing judgment and emotional reactions to parts of your life you may not feel 100% satisfied about, or parts that you deem as "broken", try to pause and reflect on what message, or should I say, opportunity, is being offered to you instead.

Go ahead and try this on your journaling page. Ask yourself:

Why DOES____ bother me so much?!
What am I making that mean? Is there something I could do differently to change my experience of that? What do I personally need in order to make that change?!
How would I know I had solved the problem?
What would be different for me?

You may already know how to do this. It's called root cause analysis and process improvement. Remember, if you keep doing what you're doing, you're going to keep getting what you're getting.

Your Life By Design

Your Life By Design

Your Life By Design

JOURNAL PROMPT

What if I shared with you that the more awareness you bring into the moment you're in, absolute full presence, the more you will enhance your productivity and outcomes in life? Presence impacts success more than any other action you could take! This means bringing your entire focus to what is happening in that moment.
How easy is that for you?

Can you practice being present? Actually looking into another person's eyes and truly LISTENING intently? All while engulfing yourself into the topic at hand? Without judgement? Or thinking about what you're going to say next? Hmmmmmmm.

And when that moment, segment, timeframe concludes...you move on and do the same again in the next moment. And the next. It isn't about the doing as much as it is a way of Being.
You. Here. Now. Present.
Then you choose.

When was the last time you experienced that level of presence and attention from someone else?
How did that feel for you?
Are you willing to try the same?

Your Life By Design

JOURNAL PROMPT

Whether your today challenges are rooted in past experiences, belief systems or down right fear, uncertainty and doubt... the truth is that's no longer relevant in the **NOW**.

Acknowledging your history, or historic way of Being, can be important but what is even more powerful is dealing with the impact that history has in your **NOW** with conscious awareness.

Sure, validate the past but keep coming back to "What do I want now?" "Historically that caused me to hesitate, but now I choose differently."
And then day after day, moment after moment consciously focusing and directing your attention, creating your story in the **NOW** enables a **life by design** in the future.

START HERE:
Am I present? Am I at choice?
Which way of thinking feels better **NOW?**

Your Life By Design

_____

_____

_____

_____

_____

_____

_____

_____

_____

_____

_____

_____

_____

_____

_____

_____

_____

_____

_____

_____

_____

_____

JOURNAL PROMPT

Practice today thinking, feeling and knowing that you deserve goodness, happiness, fulfillment.
Do you agree? Does your behavior support this belief?
If not, why do you think that is?

Deservingness blocks include feelings of guilt or embarrassment over receiving; believing that someone else will lose if you win; and thinking that receiving is selfish or egotistical.

The truth is that when you allow yourself to receive, you are balancing out your way of Being! And you have more resources available to share with others because you didn't resist receiving. Receiving is only "selfish" if it's not shared. Like simply saying 'thank you' after receiving a compliment - which validates your existence and deservingness and is actually a gift to the giver.
Think about that for a moment.

Try this powerful affirmation:
"It is safe for me to receive. I, like everyone, deserve to receive. I now allow myself to receive."

Your Life By Design

JOURNAL PROMPT

The word Equanimity derives from a Latin root that means "evenness of mind, calmness, good will, or kindness." A way of Being.

If you imagine how your body and mind feel in equanimity, they are balanced, flexible, and you feel at ease and at peace...at choice.

If you feel disappointed then move into equanimity, then you are able to consider what might be positive about a situation. If you feel irritated with someone and shift to equanimity, you can choose curiosity and ask why the person did what they did the way they did it without judging. You are in and out of perceptions like the stock market - the opportunity is to average out and find equanimity in your view to attain peace.

Equanimity allows us to keep things in proportion in life and easily shift between a variety of viewpoints and perspectives. It is an emotional state that helps us remain emotionally agile.

Equanimity is a practice. Perhaps thinking about it as a sense of balance would make it easier to access.

Where in your life are you out of equanimity or balance?

Your Life By Design

YOU DID IT

CONGRATULATIONS!

At the end of every coaching session I ask my clients: *"What is one thing you want to celebrate about yourself before we end our conversation?"*

You'd be surprised how many times, at least in the beginning of our coaching partnerships, this question stumps them.

Would it stump you? Reflect on why or why not...
How would you feel if you wrote down your accomplishments in life? What about a love letter to yourself and all the things you love about yourself not related to accomplishments? Have you looked in the mirror lately, smiled and told yourself you are beautiful, lovable, amazing?

Give yourself a break if this is hard for you. We are taught growing up that highlighting our strengths or loving ourselves out loud isn't very proper. You are not alone when it comes to hesitation here.

Celebrating oneself isn't about being braggadocios and not celebrating oneself isn't about being humble.

Learning and practicing celebrating yourself is actually demonstrating confidence in self-love. And now we know like we know that self-love fosters self-care. The necessary foundation of a life by design.

HERE YOU ARE AT THE END OF YOUR SELF-CARE COACHING JOURNAL! YOU DID IT!

How do you feel? Describe your personal experience of using this journal.

_____
_____
_____
_____
_____
_____
_____

What was the most powerful take away from this journaling experience for you?

_____
_____
_____
_____
_____
_____
_____

What is the biggest thing you learned about yourself? What would you like to learn next?

_____
_____
_____
_____
_____
_____

Your Life By Design

My Dear Friend,

Thank you. Thank you for showing up for yourself. Thank you for investing in a tool that will fundamentally change the way you see yourself forever. Thank you for realizing that you own this life of yours and that you deserve to enjoy it. Thank you for doing the work necessary to redefine the life you desire on your own terms. Thank you for remembering that the world needs you to take care of yourself so that you are happy, content and living your best life fully for everyone to see. Thank you for recognizing that you own the energy that you bring into each experience. With every smile, every laugh and every moment of soulful living you create, thank you for knowing that you make the world a better place as a result. But most importantly, thank you for being you. You are enough and you always will be. Lastly, I thank you for trusting me to hold your hand on this amazing journey to your remarkable life by design.

Happy Designing!

XOXO
Your Coach, Nicoa

REFERENCES

988 Suicide and Crisis Lifeline. Available 24 hours. English and Spanish. Or your country's mental health support hotline.

Schneider, Bruce D. (2007). Energy Leadership.

Weil, Andrew. The Relaxing Breath from Andrew Weil, M.D., also known as 4-7-8 breathing. https://www.drweil.com/videos-features/videos/breathing-exercises-4-7-8-breath/

Hay, Louise. (1998). How to Heal Your Body.

Monroe Institute. Helping people create more meaningful and joyful lives through the guided exploration of expanded consciousness. https://www.monroeinstitute.org/

Harrel, Shelly. (2021). What is Soulfulness. https://www.thesoulfulnesscenter.com/post/what-is-soulfulness

Geary, Dominique. The Antifitness Project https://theantifitnessproject.com/

WANT TO LEARN MORE?

www.coffeewithnicoa.com
Follow Nicoa on Instagram @coffeewithnicoa